Baby

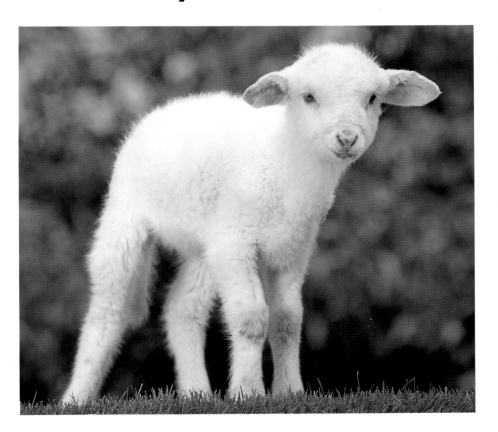

Barbara Shook Hazen

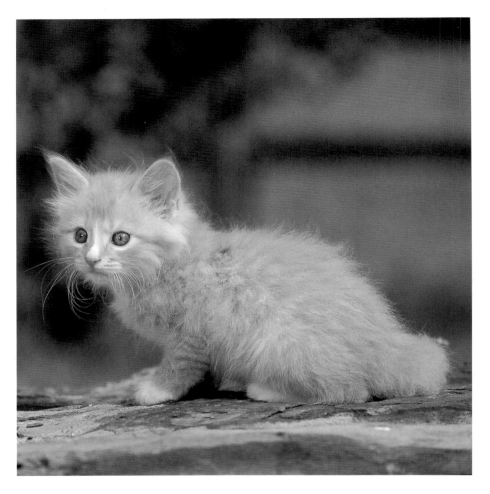

A kitten is a baby cat.

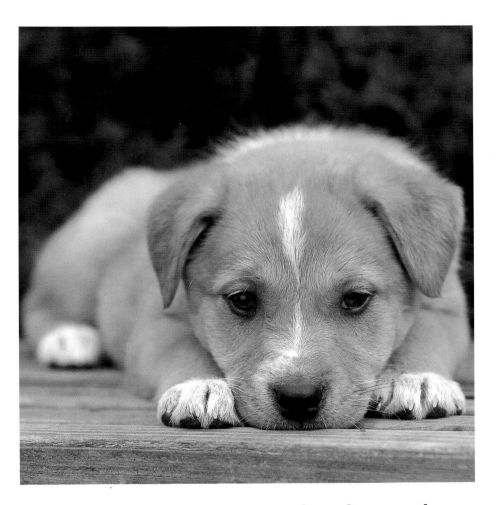

A puppy is a baby dog.

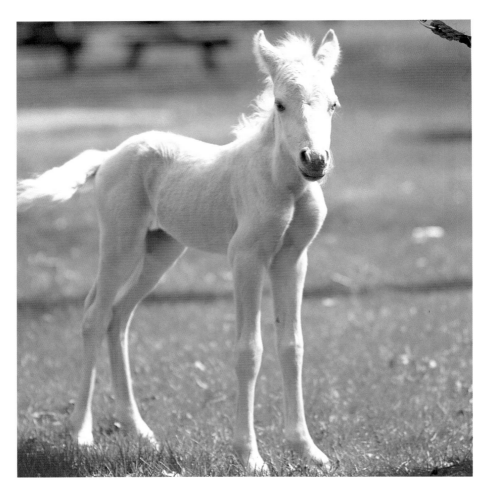

A foal is a baby horse.

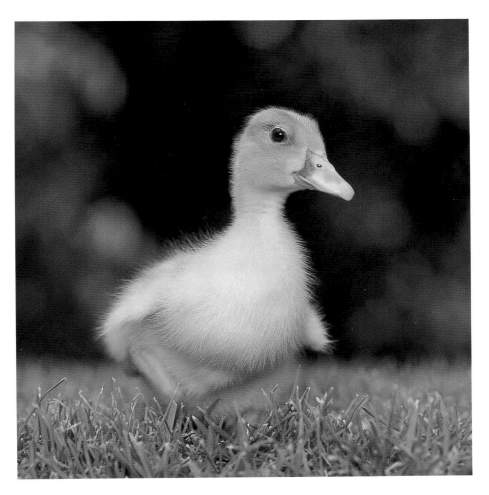

A duckling is a baby duck.

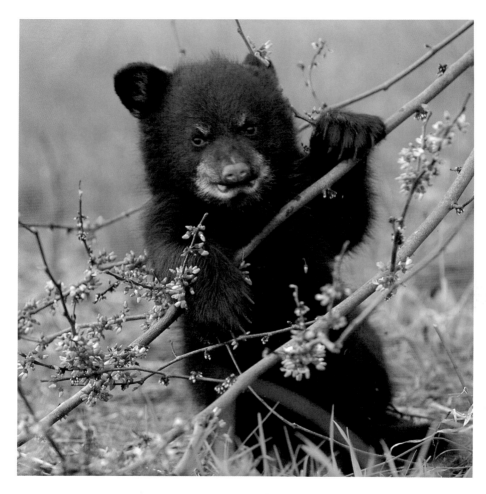

A cub is a baby bear.

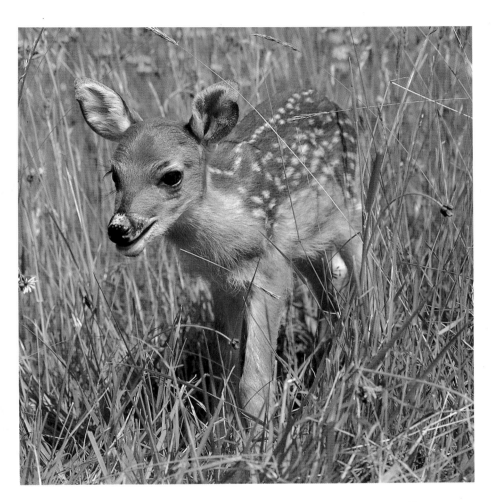

A fawn is a baby deer.

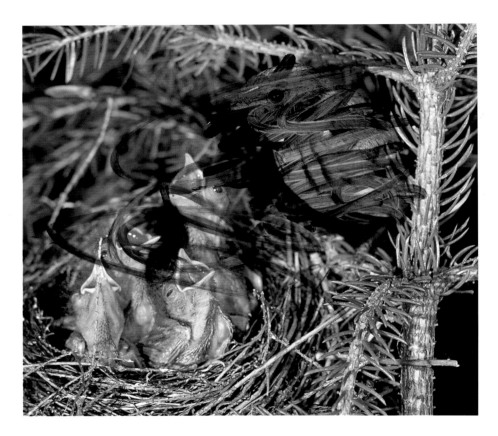

Most babies need
someone near.